WOMEN'S LACROSSE

Barron's Sports Books

Celia Brackenridge
WOMEN'S LACROSSE

Barron's
Woodbury, New York

© 1976 by Celia Brackenridge
First published in Great Britain by
Pelham Books Ltd.
52 Bedford Square
London WC1B 3EF   1976

International Standard Book No. 0-8120-5152-1

LC 77-93733

PRINTED IN THE UNITED STATES OF AMERICA

for Carole and Marge

Acknowledgements

All photographs with the exception of that on page 29 (Ken Travis) were taken by Derek Unsworth; line drawings by Roger Coombs. My thanks also to Shirley Harley and Sally Wilson for appearing in the photographs; Wycombe Abbey School for use of facilities; Len Smith's of Twickenham for uniform donated; Lady Mabel College, Yorkshire; Students in England and United States for bringing these ideas to life; and colleagues in England and the United States for fruitful discussion.

Contents

Contents

Introduction

This book is intended to show you what I believe to be an effective way of playing lacrosse. It would be foolish to state categorically that one way was correct and another incorrect since we are all different people, with different ideas, attitudes and abilities. In games we must judge a method by the success of its outcome — in other words, if it works and it is inside the rules then it is acceptable.

I shall be looking at all aspects of lacrosse in relation to the game and game situations, rather than in isolation: in this way I hope that you will see from the start how skills, practice and game are inseparably integrated.

The learning of skills and their application in the game is based on logic. Lacrosse is basically a very simple game with open boundaries and comparatively few restrictions. This means that players have multiple opportunities to use their skills and their minds creatively and independently. The absence of positional restrictions also puts a great responsibility upon the individual to cooperate sensitively with teammates.

There is only one way to learn how to play lacrosse and that is to go out and do it. My words and pictures may give you useful ideas and hints but they cannot jump into action for you, so get out and practice as often as you can. Practice is the foundation for success.

Remember that the aim of the game is to win: to win you have to score goals and that means attack, attack, attack! Every move you make should be a contribution to the attacking power of your team, whether it be a move off the ball to make way for a teammate, a direct shot at goal or a goal save and quick clearance. My concern in this book is with efficiency, economy and effective play which together add up to winning.

CHAPTER ONE

Fundamental Game Concepts

Since it is unrealistic to discuss any aspect of lacrosse without reference to the game itself I believe it is important to look first at a few of the fundamental concepts of the game.

Possession
The key to attacking play is possession and this should always be your major objective. A variety of ways of obtaining possession are available to you. When your team already has the ball, be alert to safeguarding that collective possession until such time as a shot is possible. Collective possession is maintained by accurate passing and catching as well as carrying the ball. The ball travels with a good deal more speed and less effort through the air than it will ever do in your crosse, so passing is the most economical way of moving the ball upfield. However, passing and shooting both involve deliberate loss of possession, so you must be certain that the pass or shot will be good before you risk sending the ball.

Man-to-man play
Each field player lines up beside an opponent at the start and restart of the game.

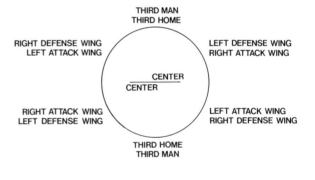

Figure 1 The field of play

The man-to-man basis of lacrosse has important implications for tactics, one of these being that, as long as play in pairs is maintained, a team is only as strong as its weakest player. In other words, as long as each defender manages to contain her own opponent no attacking progress can be made. However, as soon as one player breaks through her opponent her team has a manpower advantage, an extra player, an overlap. Once an overlap has been achieved, then the team in possession has no excuse for failing to score.

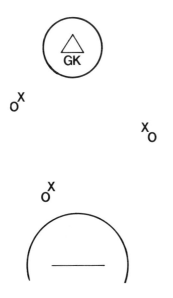
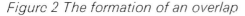
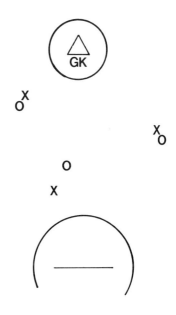

Figure 2 The formation of an overlap

The defending team employs various methods of covering an overlap to wipe out the opposition's advantage; however, the important concept to recognize at this stage is the creation and function of the overlap.

Critical areas
Critical areas are those areas of the field which are of immediate importance to the team seeking possession — that is, the defending team — because of their threat on goal. These areas vary depending on where the ball is : one permanent critical area is that surrounding the crease, particularly the ground in front of the goal.

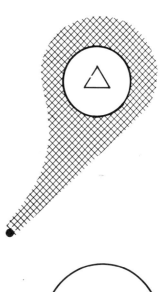

Figure 3 Critical areas of the field

Women's Lacrosse

Also critical is the actual location of the ball and any area above that point.

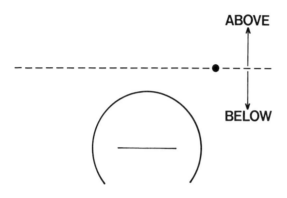

Figure 4 Points above and below the ball

Exploitation

A smart team will go out to play the opposition and not just the game. By this I mean they will organize their strategies and skills to maximize their own strengths. As an individual you will have some strengths and some weaknesses. Be proud of your strengths and use them to terrorize the opposition whenever possible, but also be aware of your own deficiencies and use practice time to improve them. Similarly, observe your opponents to find their weak spots. This may mean forcing your opponent to her weak side, making her run a lot if you think she lacks stamina, shooting in the most awkward places for the goalie to cover — these and many other considerations arise when you decide how to play a particular game. Be sure to know and use not only your strong points but also the deficiencies of your opposition.

If you want to be a clever player then I advise you also to learn the rules of the game thoroughly and consider how you may work fully within them to your own best advantage; but remember, exploiting the rules does not mean breaking them — it simply means that you use all rather than just some of the possibilities available to you.

Deception

The ability to mislead your opponent is invaluable in any game, not least in lacrosse.

Whenever possible, you and your team should use fakes, dummies and delays to confuse and deceive the opposition. The less predictable your moves the more likely they are to succeed, and this applies to both play on and off the ball.

CHAPTER TWO

Skills in the Game

Rather than discussing attacking and defending skills separately I prefer to think of all skills as attacking since they are all intended to secure and/or use possession to score goals. However, for clarity I shall refer to the team in possession as "attacks" since they are the prime movers in the game, and the team seeking possession "defenses" since they are primarily concerned to keep their goal area intact by defensive play.

Within the team each individual has a split role to play: you must be able to contribute to team progress by your work both *on* and *off* the ball.

Work on the ball involves three phases: (i) collecting; (ii) keeping; (iii) sending the ball. Work off the ball is spatial: it involves movement and positioning either to hinder the progress of the opposition or to aid the progress of your own team.

Good ball control is dependent upon competent stick handling, hence the importance of the grip and cradle.

The Grip

Since the lacrosse stick is to become your fifth limb, it is very important that you learn to hold it well. You should always have an accurate awareness of the position of the ball in your crosse,

Good grips with both top and bottom hands hold the stick upright, parallel to the body with the crosse above head height. This is your "ready position," the starting point for all skills

13

Women's Lacrosse

whether moving or still. This is achieved
by feel rather than sight and depends on a
good grip of the crosse with both hands.
Place your normal throwing hand at the
top of the crosse where the leather thongs
tie to the handle. This part of the crosse
forms a good natural handle which
discourages slipping down of the top
hand. Hold with a "trigger" grip, index
finger supporting the back of the thong
ties and thumb across the front.

Keeping both thumb and index finger
flexed avoids the problem of too much
tension in the grip. The bottom hand
holds in a "fist" grip at the very base of the
handle. Neither hand need grip too
tightly in normal play but when passing,
shooting, tackling or cradling through a
tackle the grip must be sufficiently firm
to ensure you can control the stick.

Test out your grips by carrying a ball
in a moving crosse to find the most
comfortable positions for your size of
hand. Remember that the further apart
your hands are on the crosse the more
control you have, so try to keep both
hands in place as often as possible. On
occasions one-handed catching, shooting
and picking up may be beneficial because
of lack of reach with two hands,
inflexibility or defensive pressure. Keep
your wrists and upper arms strong to cope
with these occasions — but always strive
to get both hands back on the handle as
quickly as possible to regain full control.

*The stick is pulled to the top-hand side
on the forehand cradle, still parallel with
the body and still with a trigger grip
controlling the head of the crosse. Note
that the bottom arm rests across the body
at waist height*

14

Also useful is the ability to switch hands — that is, to play with the other hand at the top — for picking up, cradling, passing and shooting. With one hand naturally dominant this is difficult to accomplish, yet it adds an invaluable dimension to your stickwork.

When pulling the stick to the backhand side during the cradle, keep the same grip. Despite a strong sideways twist of the shoulders you should be able to continue forward motion

15

Women's Lacrosse

The Cradle

Safe carrying of the ball depends on strong cradling. The cradle is a rhythmic swinging of the crosse from side to side in front of the upper body. Learn to cradle the ball on the move with your stick and body parallel and the crosse held well up. Again, for effective control, both hands should work together, the bottom hand directly below the top. Learning to cradle with stick and body in one line enables you to have good stick mobility, to take the stick to right or left keeping it close to the body for control and protection. You will rarely use an absolutely vertical cradle when running in the open game, but you may well need upright crosse mobility when in a tight spot, closely pressured by opponents.

When chased by an opponent you will find a vertical cradle particularly useful since it allows you to pull the stick across to your free side, away from trouble

16

CHAPTER THREE

Skills on the Ball

1 Collecting the Ball

Collecting the Ball from the Air – the Catch
A catch is a cradle; a cradle is a catch. Wherever the ball comes to you through the air, open the face of the crosse to it while keeping the trigger grip described earlier. Think of the catch as either a forehand or backhand cradle. All catches require a slight "give" back behind the line of ball flight. The cushion effect of this will stabilize the ball in your crosse as the full cradling motion begins. Remember that nearly always you will be pressured by a defender when taking the ball, so immediately bring the crosse to your free, unmarked side, away from trouble. Since you need so much crosse mobility for catches, your wrists should be both strong and flexible. Practice receiving the ball at all levels and on both sides of your body, then immediately bringing the crosse into a vertical cradle. Where you

Your stick is an extension of your arms and should be used to show clearly where you want to catch the ball—think of it as an inbuilt signalling system. For the forehand catch, you can see that the face of the crosse is opened to meet the ball

catch the ball will depend on where you ask to receive it (see Cutting and Indicating, p. 52). As a general rule, use two hands on the crosse for catches but be ready to reach for misplaced passes and interceptions with only one hand. For these you may choose to keep only the bottom hand on the crosse or slide the top hand (usually the stronger) down the handle and use just this. I would always prefer to see two-handed catches since they are more efficient for controlling the ball.

Useful practice can be done when learning to catch by using only one hand at the top. The turn of the upper wrist can be felt more easily this way, particularly on the backhand side. The crosse handle should stay parallel with the forearm to ensure effective control: when the bottom hand is added again, its stabilizing effect will be more fully appreciated.

Just as for a forehand catch, when the ball comes to you on the backhand side, at whatever level, treat the collection as a cradle and give gently behind the ball to absorb its momentum

Collecting the ball from the ground —the pick-up

Should the ball go on the ground you must get to it before your opponent. When the ball is either stationary or rolling away from you, keep up your running speed and bend as you approach it; get the stick down low, close to the ground and scoop. As your crosse drops, so should your head; this ensures that your knees are bent and your weight efficiently organized for control of the ball. Without this organization you could well end up playing lawn mower right across the field! The instant the ball enters the crosse, cradle it up into a vertical position — on your free side if marked. You may use just the top hand to scoop up a ground ball. This can be done on either side of you, depending on where your opponent is. Use whichever method will result in your gaining possession quickly.

Where two teammates are both chasing a ground ball from opposite directions, it should always be collected by the player toward whom it's rolling. This pick-up (sometimes called the low catch) is not only easier to collect but is also more economical since the momentum of the ball takes it into, rather than away from the crosse. The pick up is made with the crosse inverted (usually beside the feet so that they can go on running). A backward give cushions the speed of the ball. A similar collection is made for a ball which rolls across the body at an angle, although here the give will be across rather than beside the body.

These two illustrations show clearly how close the head, crosse and front foot should be to the ball as the pick-up is made. The closer the stick to your body the better your control, and the less likely you are to flick the ball up and hazard an interception by a defense. Notice, too, how the bottom hand stays low as the crosse is lifted

To meet a ground ball successfully you must turn the stick upside down beside the feet . . .

. . . this allows you to give back and cradle the ball up to the vertical while you keep on running forward

Here you can see full concentration on the ball which enters the crosse at right angles to the player's pathway. The action of collecting the ball remains the same, with speedy, close control of the ball being your prime objective

Use the controlling trigger grip for all catches, including this low one. Again, note how the stick and body are in line

Women's Lacrosse

Collecting the ball from an opponent
My motto for defense is "prevention is better than cure." It's better to stop your opponent from getting the ball than to go through the struggle of taking it from her. You can measure your effectiveness at this by observing how well you blank her out of the game – stop her from getting the ball or giving good passes, and certainly stop her from scoring.

Retaliatory skills follow this order: (a) marking and blocking the path of your opponent to prevent the pass coming to her (See p. 52); (b) intercepting the pass as it comes; (c) body checking (See p. 53); (d) stick checking; (e) blocking the pass. (a) and (c) are skills off the ball and will be considered later. (b), (d) and (e) are skills on the ball.

The Interception
There are few more satisfying skills in lacrosse than intercepting a pass. A successful interception depends not only upon a safe catching action but also on good timing, anticipation and determination. If the pass to your opponent is fast and accurate then you risk a great deal by going for the interception. However, if that pass goes the slightest bit off course you must be there to snap it up. By smart positioning you can entice your opponent to go for a ball, then accelerate at the last second to take it yourself. Once in possession of the ball, be sure to use the advantage of the overlap by setting up an attack, drawing a player and sending an accurate clearing pass. Even if you are unable to take a clean interception or pick up, you will often be close enough to your opponent to tap her stick at the moment she touches the ball. This is very disconcerting for an attack since she has no

other choice than to go for the ball. Timing of this check is critical since you risk a foul (empty crosse checking) if you go in too early.

The Stick Check
No tackle is complete until the ball is in your stick: always collect the ball from the air or the ground after you have dislodged it from your opponent's crosse. Stick checking needs close positioning to your attack while on the move – that means good footwork.

Ideally, place yourself in her path to the goal so that you continue to form a blockade at the same time as trying to gain possession. A good check dislodges the ball by short, sharp taps on the crosse. Hold your stick up with the top arm flexed and, if necessary, increase your reach by raising the bottom hand up toward your chin. The hardest part of the crosse is the wood side, so this offers the sharpest resistance for a tackle. I recommend that you tackle with the trigger grip so as to be fully prepared to follow up and collect the ball. A tackle directly in front of you gives your opponent little room to maneuver: a tackle to either side enables her more easily to pull the stick away and pass you. Make your tackles as economical as possible – sometimes an attack will cradle right into your stick if you simply hold it up above her head. The timing of your check will depend largely upon the extent to which your opponent is committed. As she goes into a dodge you have a good opportunity to check her stick. If she is on a straight run you may decide that it is better simply to contain her rather than commit yourself to a tackle and risk losing her and presenting the opposition with an overlap.

The judgement of risks and pay offs is what makes defense playing such an interesting exercise.

The defense here threatens with her stick held out in front: this helps her to keep balance as well as forcing the attack either to cradle to one side or slow down

The check jabs forward, dislodging the ball for a quick catch or pick-up by the challenger

When preparing to block a pass, watch for cues, cover the exit of the ball with your crosse . . .

The Block

When your player is about to pass you will be warned by her preparatory movement — a lift of the stick, pulling back of the shoulder (for an overarm), or a turn to the bottom hand side (for an underarm). This is your cue for a block.

As you prepare to block either an overarm or an underarm pass, align your stick parallel with hers — this is the only way you can guarantee accuracy. Block by reaching to place the back of your own crosse just beyond the top of hers as the ball is thrown.

. . . and immediately retrieve the ball to set up your own attack

Your aim is to prevent the flight of the ball and immediately follow this up by catching or picking it up, as you do after a tackle. Because of this, I favor using the trigger grip. If you turn your crosse to face hers you will not only lock your top arm but will also be unprepared to collect the ball quickly. The chances of her passing the ball directly into your crosse are very remote and do not make this discomfort worthwhile.

Again, be careful not to commit yourself by lunging early – this is just what the attacker wants as it will leave you off balance and give her a chance to dodge around you.

Women's Lacrosse

The Throw

In a throw situation you may find yourself either right or left of your opponent. Watch the umpire during the game to appraise her usual distance of throw. Be ready to sprint as soon as you hear the word "Play." You know that the ball will come to you through the air so take up a ready position with knees flexed and stick held up high. Turn the crosse slightly to left or right depending upon which side you are so that you are fully prepared to reach for the ball and pull it across to your free side as you keep on running. You may need to adapt your catching action to take a throw by cutting out the give behind the ball and instead wrapping directly around it. A throw must be taken with the players coming in toward the center of the field so you can use this to get a quick break from your opponent and set up an overlap. Before the throw, look around so that you are fully aware of your immediate options.

The Draw

The draw is often used simply as a means of initiating play but it is also a powerful tactical weapon. Although it begins with equal possession for both centers, you can create advantages from it by using a little guile.

A split stance with flexed knees gives

The English and Scottish centers face each other for a draw in the 1973 international. Notice particularly how both players keep their heads over the crosses and dip slightly, ready to push. Ready...

... Draw! The ball is pushed up and out into the air over the heads of the centers as they both extend and force their sticks up together

the best base for leverage. It is usual for the center to draw with her normal top hand at the throat of the crosse. However, the left-handed draw is mechanically more powerful since it involves a pull rather than a pushing action. For this reason, some right-handed centers switch hands just for the draw. I do not favor this unless you are also adept at catching with switched hands. Do not sacrifice any chance of positive possession at the draw. You will need to observe your opposing center a few times to assess her timing, strength and direction of push/pull. If it becomes apparent that she is able to direct the draw more accurately than you, use some deliberate placement of field players around the edge of the circle to offset her advantage. Every center plays the draw a different way. You must observe, assess and then act upon what you see to find the most likely method of controlling the ball.

The draw between two right-handers: concentration is on the ball, both centers lean over their sticks and dip slightly, ready for a strong upward push

At the draw the ball rests between the backs of the two centers' crosses which are parallel wood-to-wood at waist height

Women's Lacrosse

On the word "Draw" rotate both wrists strongly out and up forcing the ball into the air. It must go above head height to be legal but this does not mean that all your strength need go into it every time. A good center will develop a repertoire of moves at the draw which will enable her to send the ball out in any direction and at several levels, or tip it up above herself to catch. The draw is your first and most important moment for securing possession — use it wisely.

Here I have taken up a stance for a left-handed draw against a right-handed opponent. The position of the sticks is just the same: I simply move to the same side as my opponent

2 Carrying the Ball Past an Opponent

If you have no reasonable choices for a pass, or have decided to go it alone to try and create an overlap (perhaps because this is the last defender between you and a shot at goal), then you have two basic choices:

(i) The Straight Dodge
This involves a direct run at your defense, a last-minute dummy cradle to one side

followed by a quick sidestep to the other. The defense should not be able to anticipate the direction of your dodge. The intention of any dodge is to commit her, to wrong—foot her. The dummy cradle will hopefully tempt her to that side : your speed of sidestep and quick pull of the crosse back in front should leave her groping at space with you either celebrating a goal or making some constructive use of the overlap which you have just created.

The stick is pulled across at the last possible moment in a straight dodge— shown here to the left—so that the defense is kept guessing and can be wrong-footed

The author shows a strong and sudden body twist to the left, evading and wrong-footing her opponent in the 1975 international between England and the United States

Women's Lacrosse

(ii) The Roll Dodge
This dodge is harder to complete at top speed since it entails a full turn of the body and thus requires an accurate sense of balance and direction! As for the straight dodge, approach your opponent directly, giving her no clues or cues. Pull your stick to one side as you plant the foot of that same side just next to your opponent. This is your pivot foot. Swing the stick back across your body and use this cradle to turn you full circle past the defense. This dodge is very useful in "heavy traffic" situations just in front of goal.

Critical for the success of either dodge is your speedy re-alignment. Too often, I see attacks twisting right into someone, then slowing down allowing the defense to get back, close up the overlap and have another chance at tackling.

This roll dodge to the right starts in a pivot position and is followed by a complete turn out and around the defense

Women's Lacrosse

This sequence shows the pivot to the left. The front leg gives into the ground then pushes off as the crosse is swung over close to the head: the turn should immediately lead you into running in the opposite direction

The Pivot

The fastest way to change direction is a pivot. This entails placing one foot strongly forward to act as a brake, with the cross held upright and close to you on that same side. As you brake, sink the hips and bend at the knees; this lowering will both increase balance and facilitate a speedy turn. A strong pull of the crosse over the head as you restart the cradling motion will initiate the body turn toward the back foot. The front brake foot now becomes the back power foot. A strong extension of the legs pushes the body off into running again.

To use a pivot effectively in the game you must be aware of what is going on directly behind you. You use it to bring wide play back toward the center of the field, or, more commonly, to lose a close-marking defense, perhaps immediately following a ground pick up or a catch.

You must be competent at both left and right pivots since you can be marked on either side of the body.

When closely chased from behind after a dodge or a pivot, a slightly weaving run will prevent your opponent from passing you or reaching your stick easily.

33

3 Sending the Ball

Sending the Ball to a Teammate—Passing
Where a teammate is better placed than you to advance the attack then you should pass the ball to her. You will probably be approaching a defender or running alongside one as you are about to pass. Few advantages are to be gained from passing if you are free in open play. Opinions vary as to the best method of passing the ball. I advise you to set yourself up, whatever pass you choose, by keeping your feet on the move—cover forward territory as long as possible before passing off.

The Overarm Pass
The overarm pass is probably the most direct and usually the most accurate passing action. It is based on the overarm throwing action, which is why you are recommended to place your normal throwing hand at the top of the crosse. Together with the sidearm pass, it is the only skill in lacrosse which requires a major alteration of top hand grip. The crosse turns in the fingers of the top hand so that the palm is behind the throw. The face of the crosse is not completely open but rests at an angle to the target. I believe you can only be 100 per cent sure of accuracy in overarm passing if you line up both hands with your target. This means you must turn the upper body to the top hand side and take your bottom hand across to that side to prepare for a throw straight forwards. Aim with the butt of the stick and use a combined pull/push action to direct the ball toward the target. Follow through until the bottom hand finishes right under the top arm: the top arm and stick handle should then be parallel. The height of your pass will be

The slight change of top-hand grip here opens the face of the crosse for the overarm pass. Notice also the aiming hand and elbow lift of the bottom arm

determined by the height of your follow through.

Whatever the distance of the pass the action always remains the same. For effective control the ball should leave the crosse at the very top: this makes the most of available leverage and ensures lift and flight for the pass. One of the reasons for a preparatory cradle before the pass is to

34

As the stick follows through toward the target, the bottom hand is pulled up under the top arm

The Sidearm Pass

This is a more difficult pass to direct since there is always a chance that the ball will leave the crosse at a tangent to the required direction. The action is very similar to that of the overarm pass, utilizing a snap leverage of the bottom hand. However, the top hand moves around at shoulder level or below to keep the flight of the ball low. This can be used to pass around or under the arm of a defender or where you do not have room to lift the stick up for an overarm.

The end of the sidearm pass also points the stick toward the target and leaves the stick and top arm parallel

swing the ball up to the top part of the crosse so that it leaves cleanly and does not stick. A pass which falls short of the target has probably come from the lower baggy area of the crosse. In a good cradling action the ball will always be moving freely in the upper part of the crosse. Practice exaggerated cradling and check that you can achieve this.

The Reverse Pass

This pass is executed with the trigger grip. It sends the ball to the top-hand side or backwards of you. Take the head of the crosse to the backhand side, aim with the

35

Women's Lacrosse

butt of the stick again, lining up both hands with your target. Snap down with the bottom hand as you lift and extend the top. This is most accurate over short distances and is a useful quick feed off pass in the game.

For a good reverse pass, keep the crosse very high throughout. A common fault is to let the ball drop too early and lose flight. As the reverse pass follows through, the stick and top arm are again in line

The underarm pass can send the ball either forward or across you. After a cradle to the backhand side, the crosse head drops as the top and bottom hands change places in space

The Underarm Pass

As with other passes, the underarm or shovel pass ends with both hands in line with the target. Keep your cradling grip throughout the pass. Prepare by taking the stick across to the backhand side in a vertical cradle; instead of then swinging it back high across the body, the head of the crosse should continue to drop and circle around toward the target. This pass can be used either forwards or to the top-hand side of you. It is less direct than the overarm pass but is useful when a marker prevents you preparing for other passes on the top-hand side.

The stick head is swung toward the target. Notice the grips have not altered. This pass is at medium level but could be sent higher or lower by varying the finish of the follow through

37

Women's Lacrosse

Choosing Your Pass

The kind of pass you use will depend on several factors: (*a*) which side are you marked? (*b*) how far away is help? (*c*) which side of you is help? (*d*) how much time do you have to send the ball? The overarm is the most versatile since it can be used over virtually any required distance and at any level. The other passes are harder to control accurately but can be both effective and very quick, particularly the sidearm.

Another way of sending the ball to a teammate is the flick. This involves simply lifting or flicking a ground ball up from or along the floor. This is very handy to use when you are scrapping with an opponent to pick up the ball, or if you are chasing a ground ball and see a teammate close by ready to help out. The flick can save you a great deal of time and energy.

Sending the Ball to the Goal — Shooting

Shooting in lacrosse can be either play or display. As a shooter your only concern should be with denting the back of the net, so shoot to score not just to look pretty! There are many varied shooting techniques and all of them will succeed with an empty net in practice, but not all of them are functional in game situations. Remember that when shooting you are deliberately conceding possession, so your lead up to a shot should place you in the best possible position to score. Very often a shot is made to look spectacular because the shooter gets herself into all kinds of difficult situations before getting the shot away. This is not good attack play.

Shots arise from two basic situations: one where you carry the ball into the critical area in front of goal, the other where you receive it there and make an immediate shot. If you make a shooting cut to receive the ball in front of goal, try to cut down the number of cradles preceding your shot to the absolute minimum — to none, if possible. If you carry the ball into this area, try to disguise your shot as the goalkeeper's attention will have been on you all this time.

The Overarm Shot

This is probably the most powerful shooting action and for that reason is the one most frequently used. It can certainly be both quick and accurate although I would always encourage you to sacrifice power for accuracy. Once you have achieved precision in your shot, then you may think about speeding it up, but not until then. The good shooter is able to control not only the power but also the line and level of the shot. This means that the ball is directed accurately toward the target and flighted well to arrive at the right height. To achieve accuracy of line, the same points apply as for the overarm pass. Cradle the crosse high and back on the top-hand side, bring the lower hand over to that side, aim with the butt of the stick forward and line up both hands with the target. Keep both hands in that alignment throughout the shot and follow through.

Accuracy of level in an overarm shot is determined by the point of release and the height of the follow through. Finish a high shot with the stick above the head; a medium shot with the stick at about waist height; and a ground or bounce shot with the stick head almost touching the ground in front of you.

All overarm shots, including the high shot, are based on a downward pull of the

The preparation for the overarm shot does not differ from the beginning of the overarm pass but you may choose to lift the crosse higher. The bottom arm pulls through strongly in this shot

The finish of the shot is low to the ground, pointing toward the target. This enables you to send the ball with both speed and accuracy

stick. This is why it is so important that you prepare with the stick high. The double leverage of top and bottom hands catapults the ball from the stick. As you pull the stick over and down, also reach forward.

Power is achieved by a combination of speed and force. Again, a high lift gives you plenty of room both to build up speed before the release of the ball, and to use the dual leverage which forces the ball from the crosse. The high preparatory cradle gives the defense a hint that you are about to shoot, so you may choose to disguise the shot by delaying, turning or veering to one side.

The Reverse Overarm Shot
This skill resembles exactly the reverse overarm pass (see p. 35). Its great advantage is that it enables you to send the ball from high on the backhand side, often surprising the goalkeeper and defenses who think you are unable to get a shot away from here. The shot is usually used when approaching or crossing the goalmouth, fairly close to the crease, and can direct the ball either low or high.

The Sidearm Shot
This is a very powerful shot with a heavy stress on the top-hand side. Use the same action as for the sidearm pass and remember that the height of your follow through will determine the level of your shot. This action can be used to skid the ball very effectively into the goal on a slippery surface.

The High Shot
Although the rules do not allow shots to be placed unnecessarily high and hard at the goal, the frame is six feet high, so you

would be foolish to exclude high shots from your shooting repertoire. High shots are most often used close to goal. Be careful that you do not step or reach over the crease before, during or after the shot since this will result in a foul, a wasted effort and immediate loss of possession to the goalkeeper — what a gift for her! As for the bounce shot, prepare high since you should direct the ball downwards rather than lifting it into the goal. Snappy wrist action with both arms should float the ball to your chosen target.

The Underarm Shot
The underarm shot is commonly used by a player crossing the goalmouth from right to left wing. It differs little from the underarm pass except that the preparation is more strongly away from the target to allow more room for a build-up of power and speed towards goal. Also, the follow through is low. A rising underarm shot is dangerous and will almost certainly be called foul by the umpire. The underarm is both easy to detect and easy to stop so I would recommend that you use it only when time and space demand.

Choosing Your Shot
As for passes, the kind of shot you use will depend on the situation. However, always keep in mind the risk you incur by sending the ball so try to use shots which have a high success rate.

This means that you must work hard to give yourself room for such shots and time to place them carefully. Quick shots following a pass are more likely to upset the opposition than shots from a long distance runner! Remember that waist-high shots and corner shots are the most

Notice that the top hand palm is behind the crosse at the start of this high shot. The stick is lifted high so the placement can be made down into the goal

difficult for a goalkeeper to save and that ground conditions can help you either to bounce or skid the ball at an awkward angle for her to recover.

Your effectiveness as a shooter will depend very much upon your attitude in the game. A goal-hungry attack will not only get through to goal more frequently but will also enjoy the deserved pleasure of scoring. At all times remember
—GO FOR GOAL
—GO HARD
—BE A THREAT
then you'll be a winner!

CHAPTER FOUR

Crease Play

As a mark of respect for goalkeepers and the work that they do I have chosen not to hide this section away at the end as happens in so many coaching books.

As goalkeeper you are the first line of attack on your team: you are both the fire and the thermometer of team spirit. As with field players, think of your contribution to play in terms of three phases — collecting, keeping and sending the ball. However, the shorter the middle phase the better since your greatest threat to the opposition is by setting up a fast break which can build in an overlap advantage for your team at the very start of the move.

Your stance will be a matter for personal preference; either feet together, or together but slightly split forward/back. Either way, a little flexion at the knees will help the resilience and balance you need for quick and steady moving around the goalmouth.

Hold the crosse down and forward of your body using the trigger grip: the crosse is your first line of defense and your body, the second. Taking a catch directly in front of you is not only difficult but also uncomfortable. However, to offer the strongest resistance to shooting power you must line up this way.

The ready position of the goalkeeper — here using a feet together stance — must be balanced and keep the stick ahead of the body. The crosse is held down because the instinctive reaction when facing a shot is to lift, not lower. Notice again the trigger grip to allow shots to be caught and the slipped bottom hand which increases the close mobility of the crosse

43

The split stance in this illustration keeps your weight forward, an important factor for positive goalkeeping

Mobility is a must for the goalkeeper. Do all stickwork practices in pads (and a mask if you normally wear one) until you are as agile as any other player. Your stickwork must not only be failsafe but also very quick since the speed of your clearance can determine the success or failure of an attack at the other goal.

Before a game, warm up with a chosen teammate who will give you the shots *you* want. At all costs avoid setting yourself up in front of a firing squad! Once the game starts, follow the play wherever it is by moving across the goalmouth with small steps around a semi-circular path. If the ball is out to the right, whether near or far, then be sure to cover the post on that side. Not an inch of space should

When covering the play, stand close to the near post. By moving across the goalmouth in a semi-circle you effectively narrow the angles available to the shooter. Here there is very little to aim at !

show to the ball player. As play moves from wing to wing, follow it with full concentration. For a head-on attack you may prefer to stand slightly to the left of center because your reach to the top-hand side is greater. This entices shots to your stronger side.

When the ball is behind the crease, cover the post on that side. As the ball player approaches the front area she should be forced toward the crease edge by your closest defense, so that together you can double team her.

Be ready to call instructions to your own defense at any time. This not only directs them but also reassures them and keeps them orientated to the goal location without constantly having to look around.

45

Women's Lacrosse

Keep both hands on your stick in the ready position, sliding the bottom hand up a little for closer control. One-handed play (with the top hand only) can be very effective for close shots, especially if you move your top hand right up behind the crosse so that it becomes like a large glove in your hand. You may block or catch with the other hand — but must be sure to place the ball immediately in your crosse for a speedy clearance. For the majority of shots, especially those from farther out, keep both hands on the stick and use it to take the shot as a catch. If a catch is not possible, then block the shot — accept that your first priority is to stop a goal being scored. This is particularly true of a shot high on the left where you may well be unable to turn the crosse in time for a regular backhand catch. In this case block the ball with the back of the crosse.

When a player is about to shoot you usually get some kind of cue. For overarm shots this is a lift up and back with the top hand; a high cradle may also precede the shot. With underarm shots there is a strong turn away from goal as the elbow of the top arm tucks firmly into the side before the shot is unleashed.

Watch carefully for this wind up as it will vary from player to player. You should always look out for "favorites" of the opposing attacks and encourage your own players to block out a shooter on her stronger side. Your line-up for all shots should take account of the shooting angles available. The closer to the front edge of the crease that you are positioned the narrower the shooting angle. You must entice the shooter to place the ball where you can most easily take it. For shots close to goal, be careful that you do not come out too far and allow the shooter to put the ball over or around you. For longer shots, place yourself at right angles to the shooter's stick: you may need to take the ball before, after or on the bounce and should judge your forward movement according to its flight. The underarm shot is probably the easiest shot to stop since it entails a large wind-up and is usually taken close to goal. As soon as you spot the shot coming, move to the edge of the crease to block it with your stick in front of your flexed knees. Close high shots are also easily predicted and can be stopped by an advancing goalkeeper. You can improve the accuracy of your block by getting your top hand well up behind the crosse.

If possible take the ball into a cradle and back for a clearance in one action. Keep a constant eye out for your own players so that you can clear as soon as a shot is saved. Dogma is dangerous in coaching but I am dogmatic about the goal clear: it must go to the side of the field away from the critical area in front of the crease. It is suicide to pass forward and risk a second onslaught on the goal. Clearance from the side of the goal ensures a run up and an unhampered throw. Your defense players should have a working relationship with you, which means that they are ready to take a clearing pass at any time by cutting to the side of the field, near or far from goal.

The moment a shot is made, the break out for a clear should be started upfield and away from the goal. Also part of that working relationship is an agreement of your wishes about vision. As the punch-bag for the shot, you have the prerogative to choose how far your team mates interfere with the shooting action. Some goalkeepers like a defense to keep up

Clearing from the side of the cage protects the crosse and gives room for an unhampered throw. Here the sideways stance is preparing the body for a strong forward push. Notice how the top arm has dropped below shoulder level at the back — this is so that the pass may be sent up high over the heads of the opposition attack

Thrust your weight on to the front leg and as the clear follows through end with both hands and the crosse in line with the top arm. The high finish ensures high flight of the ball

Bounce shots taken on the half volley like this should be closely backed up by the legs. With this compact body shape and weight forward the goalkeeper is well prepared to stop even the most powerful shot cleanly. Notice the goalkeeper has come forward to kill the bounce. Note, too, the catching grip: good wrist work is essential to capture the ball as there is not always room for a large backward give of the crosse

As soon as you spot the underarm shot coming, step right out to the front edge of the crease. Keep your weight well forward over the ball so that any rebounds are directed down rather than out into the field again

constant tackling pressure, others prefer a clear view of the complete shooting action (which is less likely to be deflected). You must decide for yourself what you want and work out a general rule with your defense players.

Although your homing instinct should keep you within the protection of the crease, you must be ready to go for any passes or wide shots which come within reach of the crease. Remember that prevention is better than cure, so try to cut out the last pass to goal. When out of the crease you cannot take the ball back in, so go positively and get that ball! Once out, you have created an overlap, therefore use it sensibly and draw a defender before clearing. I would love to see a goalkeeper go right up through the field and score at the other end. In theory there is nothing to stop this — see if you can make it happen in reality!

The high shot can be blocked by either the back or face of the crosse. Notice that the goalkeeper has aligned her stick with mine to be sure of an accurate block. She has also come right out to the crease edge to narrow my shooting possibilities

CHAPTER FIVE

Skills off the Ball

By the law of averages each player on a team can expect to be involved on the ball for only a matter of seconds in any one game. Therefore, for a team to make good use of collective possession, those attacks without the ball must ensure that their moves create the best set-up for the ongoing movement of the ball itself. Moves off the ball by the defending team are all concerned with containing progress by the opposition and inducing a turnover of possession.

By a sudden change of direction the attack leaves me off balance and signals clearly for a pass. The attack always has a slight advantage over me because she initiates moves I must follow

Offensive Skills

Getting Free
This is the preparatory phase to cutting for a pass. If you succeed in losing your opponent, you should be able to make a clearer cut and an easier catch. To be free from a marker can mean several different things. If your team is able to use precision passing you will need very little room in which to "free" yourself for a catch—just a stick-head's advantage over your opponent. Mind you, this demands great skill. I would say that you are free from a defense as soon as you have committed her in some way, perhaps to overstepping in one direction. You achieve this commitment by the use of dodges and feints with the body and/or by change of position of your stick—for example, from high to low, or from left to right.

Women's Lacrosse

Cutting and Indicating

Once free from your opponent, immediately cash in on the situation by making a cut. Cuts are used for two basic reasons: either to help out the ball player, or to take the pass preceding a shot. Helping cuts are best made to the free side of the ball player where she can both see you and get the ball out to you easily. Shooting cutters should try to position the crosse so that the give of the catch becomes the preparation for the shot. This "quickstick" shot at goal eliminates cradling and can deceive the goalkeeper by its speed.

As you cut for the ball, use your stick as a signal to indicate where you wish to receive the pass. A clear indication is worth a thousand calls. Place your stick where you can most easily take the ball out of reach or your opponent. This will probably be toward the space that you have just created by getting free and will also depend upon whether your opponent is tall or short, right- or left-handed.

Circulating

Movement by the offensive team should be continuous but constructive. If you are above the ball, you need constant awareness of your positioning in relation to three critical points — the ball, the goal and your opponent. Distance from your fellow attacks is generally advisable since it allows you to see and move more freely.

The upfield surge of an attacking move should keep you peeling around to get ahead of the ball, thus maintaining the numbers advantage of your own team. By circulating as the ball comes upfield you create spaces for your own use and uncertainty for your opposing defense.

Either side of the advancing ball player are free spaces into which helping cuts can be made. If the forward direction is blocked by a defense then this is where the attacks should be making cuts

2 Defensive Skills

Marking

Your first intention as a marking player is to prevent your opponent from receiving the ball. If you watch the player carefully you should be able to anticipate where she will want to make a move and then block out her cutting path. This will certainly upset her timing and may also keep her out of the play long enough to leave her below the ball.

Since lacrosse passes can go over your head, it is risky for you to stand in front of your opponent thinking that this positioning blocks her from the ball. If you are taking up a tight man-to-man marking position, stand with your body between your opponent and your goal and your stick between her and the ball. This way you give yourself a chance of moving around for an interception if the pass is bad but you are there as a physical blockade should a good pass come to her. Don't be tempted offside if the approaching pass is good.

Loose marking is less effective than close man-to-man marking when you are playing an equally strong team or at the moment that the ball comes near your opponent. However, it has advantages in that it leaves you with slightly longer in which to size up likely dodges and it makes your opponent move further with the ball in order to get around you. Loose marking can be a useful means of forcing lateral play and thus of stalling a threat on goal.

Body Checking

Should you either concede the pass to your opponent or fail to make an interception then your next line of defense is body checking. As she runs toward you, begin to shadow her body and her stick with yours, lining up stick on stick. You will never be able to move backwards as fast as the ball player running forwards but you may be able (*i*) to force her off her path to goal; (*ii*) to force her to pass; (*iii*) to force an error.

It is imperative that you do not allow her to pass you with the ball since this immediately sets up a numerical superiority for her team.

Double Teaming

By keeping on your opponent's stick you should be able to dictate her dodges and perhaps even induce her to move toward another of your teammates. The two of you are then double teaming — working as a pair to sandwich the ball player. Double teaming is a high risk strategy since it leaves the opposition with an extra player, an overlap. However, it should also be a successful strategy since two on to one gives you a good chance of gaining possession.

Pressing

When you are short of time in a game and are behind in score, it becomes important for you to force a turnover of possession. As a group, you and your fellow defenses can press the attacks by extremely tight marking and harassing of the ball player. Your intention is to force an error from the attacks which will give you possession. Working this close to them is risky since they can very easily sidestep to make an overlap but in a press situation you have nothing to lose.

CHAPTER SIX

Using the Field

1 Setting up a Group Attack

Group attack stems from individual possession of the ball either at the draw or following a turnover in midfield. The quickest route to goal is a straight line and while forward speed is maintained by the ball player, her teammates should keep out of her path to goal by circulating in the offensive area above the ball. By keeping above the ball they remain a potential threat to the opposition and keep up the numbers on their own team. As the ball player draws a defender, she should pass off to one of these fellow attacks. If you are an attack player above the ball, cut only when the ball player is pressured or when your defender is drawn off.

If forward speed is reduced because of defensive harassment, then helping cuts should be made to the free side of the ball player. This may well involve moving the ball away from goal or across the field until an opening for an overlap is created. It is at this stage that a change of pace in the attack can be so valuable: a sudden acceleration as the overlap is initiated will increase the effect of the attack. Lateral or square passing does not penetrate the critical shooting area which the defense is trying to protect, but it may well be used,

together with a quick through or straight pass, as a ploy to create an overlap. Lateral thrust is useful nearer to goal as a means of stretching a containing defense. By using the full width of the field you put the defense on the rack and keep them constantly guessing about your angle of approach to goal.

The most difficult attack for a defense to cover is one which penetrates the center of the field from a fast break. For this reason, avoid bringing the ball all the way upfield on one side. If a defense clearance is taken on the wing, move the ball into the center of the field to increase opposition uncertainty.

Should a fast break fail to reach the goal before the defense has time to amass, an alternative method of attack may be required. This is when your second weapon, that of constantly switching direction, comes into play. When facing a zone formation or a loose man-to-man defense, try to entice the defenders to come out and take the ball from you, rather than taking it directly to them or trying to pass it over them. Always aim to commit the defense and then use the opening that this commitment creates.

The area behind the crease can profitably be used to set up quick passing plays and cause constant switching of attention by the defensive players, including the goalkeeper. Fast, direct passing between the attacks should keep the defenses guessing and may tempt them to become committed, off balance or out of position. This is when you should sting hard and never miss an opportunity to put the ball in the net.

2 Setting up a Group Defense
Successful group defense depends not only on skill but also on determined cooperation by all players seeking possession. Three basic defensive systems are available to your team. Common to all is the idea that once possession is lost, *every* player in the team must adopt a defensive role.

(i) The Man-to-Man Defense
This is the basic and most usual method of cover. Each player is individually responsible for containing her own opponent by close marking on goal-side/ball-side. Each should be strong and capable in her personal defensive skills. Should any single opposing player break through and get goal side of her defense with the ball, either by dodging or by sheer speed, then the attacking team has an extra player, an overlap.

To obliterate this threat, Cover Point comes off Second Home to take the extra attack. Meanwhile, the nearer of the two Defense Wings drops in to cover Second Home, thus leaving the free player on the wing, in the least dangerous place. All this time the originally beaten defense speedily attempts to make up ground and pick up the free player. The timing of Cover

Point's move off Second Home is crucial: she must be confident that her Defense Wings are sufficiently close to cover Second Home. The Defense Wings operate on an arc-shaped pathway similar to covering fullbacks in orthodox hockey. If the ball is coming down one wing, the Defense Wing on that side marks up close to her opponent. The Defense Wing furthest from the ball drops off her opponent and hovers on a level with Second Home, ready for the interchange or switch. Once a switch has occurred, the defenses should remain with their new opponents until the ball is safely cleared and there is time enough for them to move back to their original opponents.

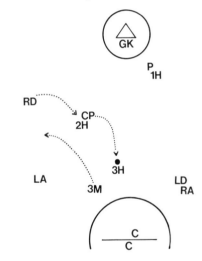

Figure 5 An example of the Defense Wing interchange. Third Home has passed Third Man with the ball, thus creating an overlap. Cover Point takes Third Home; Right Defense Wing takes Second Home: Third Man attempts to get back and pick up Left Attack Wing

This type of defense should be used against either unknown opposition or opposition of comparable strength to your own.

Women's Lacrosse

(ii) The Helping Defense

This defense is useful against a team with a high-scoring attack. Defenders mark on a very close man-to-man basis but overload their cover by bringing back into the defending end either one or two helpers from the midfield. For example, the two Defense Wings may drop back and their regular places taken by their own Attack Wings. It is therefore possible for the defense to use an extra cover or sweeper to double team the ball player. This usually results in a turnover of possession as such harassment easily forces errors. Should a second sweeper be used, she attempts to pick off interceptions from the passes of the harassed ball player.

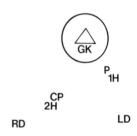

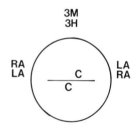

Figure 6 Example of line-up for a helping defence; Right Attack marks opposing Left Attack and Left Attack marks Right Attack

Again, players stay until a clearance is made. Since few attacks will now be upfield to receive the ball, it may be necessary to build up numbers in attack by two or three defenses carrying the ball upfield using square passes and becoming attacks. This is a versatile system which shares the workload of attack and defense more evenly than the strict man-to-man arrangement.

(iii) The Zone Defense

A zone defense is a sophisticated system of play based on the acceptance by one team that they are facing a very much stronger opposition. The aims of a zone are to contain the opposition, to reduce scoring and to force errors. Zone players do not go out and seek the ball but let it come to them.

Instead of attending closely to one player zone defenders attend to the ball. They watch it constantly and orientate to it. They mark or cover a specific area rather than a person; for example, the four corners of a square in front of goal.

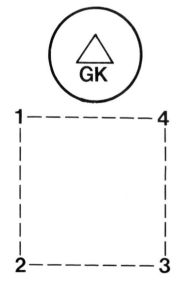

Figure 7 A box zone

In this way they protect the critical shooting area. Attacks cannot hurt a team until they get into this area, so a wise defense forces the opposition to keep playing laterally *around* the zone. This is done by double-teaming the ball player. For example, a fifth defense, the pivot, moves about the front of the zone facing the ball. Each corner player slides down one as the ball is passed around, as in the diagrams.

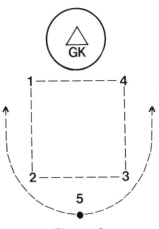

Figure 8a

Figure 8a–e An attack "horseshoe" kept at bay by a zone defense

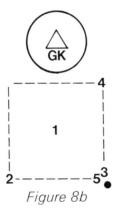

Figure 8b

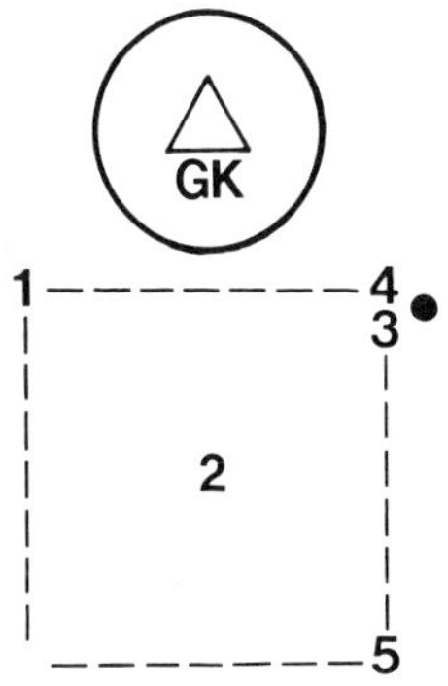

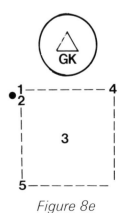

Figure 8c

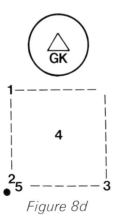

Figure 8d

Figure 8e

Women's Lacrosse

The corner player farthest from the ball sags into the middle of the zone, again hoping to pick off any attempted passes across the zone. The whole intention of the zone is to force lateral passes: should the ball player be tempted to pass across the zone then her pass, unless very quick, direct and well-disguised is likely to be intercepted. The goalkeeper, who can see the whole field of play, may direct operations by giving instructions to her zone.

Zones can certainly be negative and do require a team to concede a good deal of midfield territory in order that they have time to form. However, they can be most effective in thwarting a consistently strong opposition.

With a repertoire of these three defensive systems you should become much more versatile as a group and as individuals. You should look at a match not just as a game of lacrosse but as a contest against a specific opposition. One hopes you'll be able to select and adjust your formations to cope with the strengths and weaknesses in the personnel of both your own and the opposite team.

It should always be remembered that the fundamental intention of any defense is to stop scoring. Gaining possession from the opposition is a desirable bonus and enables immediate reversal of roles from defense to attack. A versatile defense is far more likely to succeed than a stereotyped one.

CHAPTER SEVEN

Making the Most of Practice Time

Any beginner can quickly sample the thrills of a lacrosse game with even the most elementary grasp of stickwork skills. Through playing in games and gamelike situations players come to see both the relevance of stickwork practice and the patterns of play which utilize these skills.

Stickwork and game can never truly be separated although we tend to spend time specifically working on stickwork. This time is well spent since the effectiveness of any tactic in the game depends upon the stickwork skills of the players in the team. As your stickwork improves, you will gain in confidence and find that you are able to concentrate more on the strategies of play and worry less about keeping the ball in your crosse.

For practice time to be most beneficial always remember the following:
1. to have a focus, a direction of play, a goal;
2. to have an opponent (lacrosse begins on a man-to-man basis);
3. to base your practice on a game situation by allocating positions to those involved and by discussing its application to the game;
4. to use both sides of the body, for example, dodge right and left, catch on right and left;
5. to practice a sensible sequence of events, for example, add a clearing pass on to the end of a practice for interceptions;
6. to work at top speed — rest between practices but never during them!

Your practices may not always satisfy all these conditions — indeed in the early stages of skill learning you will almost certainly have to work more slowly and without the pressure of a worrying defender. However, as you become more confident and more adept you should aim to incorporate all these conditions to make your practices truly realistic.

Skill Chains

The game of lacrosse has been considered in terms of skill on and off the ball. Individual practice should be based on chains of these skills built up by combining realistic sequences. A skill chain on the ball might be: Catch . . . . Dodge . . . . Pass. The same chain further elaborated could be: Catch (high, medium or low) . . . . Dodge (left or right) . . . . Pass (overarm or underarm) or any variation of this. Your focus in practice might be on only one link of the chain but the rest should always be included to give fluency and relevance to the practice.

59

Women's Lacrosse

Skill chains can be increased in difficulty along various dimensions:

Speed	Slow moving	Full speed
Opposition	Passive	Active
Complexity	General tasks	Specific tasks
Length	3 . . . 4 . . . 5 . . . 6 . . . etc:	number of links

(The more links in the chain, the closer you approximate to a real game situation.)

Conditioning

All the lacrosse skill and knowledge in the world will be little use unless you are physically fit. Physical preparation can take many forms but, as with practice, relate your conditioning to the demands of the game.